CODE YOUR OWN JUNGLE ADVENTURE

CODE WITH CAPTAIN MARIA IN THE CITY OF GOLD

Quarto is the authority on a wide range of topics.

Quarto educates, entertains and enriches the lives of
our readers—enthusiasts and lovers of hands-on living.

www.quartoknows.com

Author: Max Wainewright
Illustration and design: Henry Smith
Designer: Adrian Morris
Editor: Claudia Martin

First published in the UK in 2017
by QED Publishing
Part of The Quarto Group
The Old Brewery, 6 Blundell Street
London, N7 9BH

A catalogue record for this book is available from the British Library.

ISBN 978 1 78493 840 6

Printed in China

Scratch is developed by the Lifelong Kindergarten Group at MIT Media Lab.
See: http://scratch.mit.edu

INTERNET SAFETY

Children should be supervised when using the Internet,
particularly when using an unfamiliar website for the first time.
The publishers and author cannot be held responsible for the content
of the websites referred to in this book.

INFORMATION ON RESOURCES

You can use Scratch on a PC or Mac by opening your web browser
and going to: http://scratch.mit.edu
Then click 'Try it out'.

There is a very similar website called 'Snap', which also works on iPads.
It is available here: http://snap.berkeley.edu/run

If you want to run Scratch without using the web, you can download it from here:
http://scratch.mit.edu/scratch2download/

CONTENTS

USING SCRATCH

In this book, we will use a computer language called Scratch to code our games. It's free to use and easy to learn. Before you set off on your expedition with Captain Maria, take a few minutes to get to know Scratch.

FINDING SCRATCH

To start using Scratch, open up a web browser and click in the address bar. Type in **scratch.mit.edu** then press **'Return'**. Click **'Try it out'**.

STARTING SCRATCH

To code a computer game, you need to tell your computer exactly what to do. You do this by giving it commands. In Scratch, commands are shown in the form of 'code blocks'. You build a game by choosing code blocks and then joining them together to create a program.

Your Scratch screen should look like this:

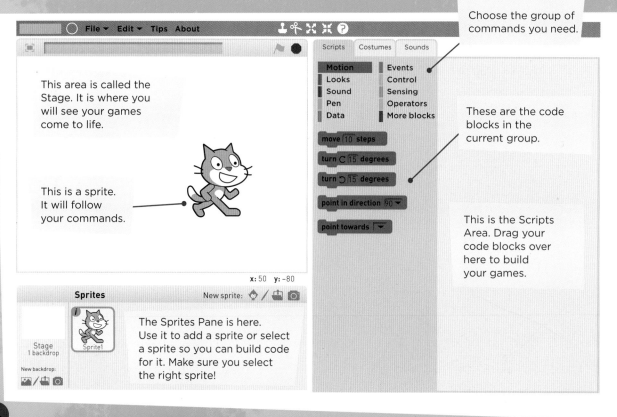

Choose the group of commands you need.

This area is called the Stage. It is where you will see your games come to life.

This is a sprite. It will follow your commands.

These are the code blocks in the current group.

This is the Scripts Area. Drag your code blocks over here to build your games.

The Sprites Pane is here. Use it to add a sprite or select a sprite so you can build code for it. Make sure you select the right sprite!

USING CODE BLOCKS

Before you drag out any code blocks, try clicking on one to make the cat sprite move forwards ...

... or rotate 15 degrees.

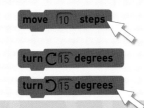

Click in the white boxes (which are shown in this book as coloured) then type different numbers to change how far the sprite moves or turns.

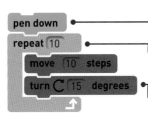

Now try dragging code blocks over to the Scripts Area and joining them together. Click on one of the blocks to run the whole program.

You can break code blocks apart, but you need to start with the bottom block if you want to separate them all. To remove a code block, drag it off the Scripts Area.

move 20 steps
turn C 15 degrees
move 80 steps
turn C 15 degrees

Use the colour of the code blocks to work out which group you will find the block in. It will also give you a clue about what the code block will do.

pen down

repeat 10
    move 10 steps
    turn C 15 degrees

Get the **'Pen down'** block from the green **Pen** group.

The **'Repeat'** block is a mustard colour, so it's in the **Control** group.

The blue code blocks are in the **Motion** group.

USING THE DRAWING AREA

To draw a new sprite, click on the **Paint new sprite** button located in the top bar of the **Sprites Pane**.

To draw a backdrop for the Stage, click on the **Stage** button located in the **Sprites Pane** then click on **Paint new backdrop** underneath it.

The **Drawing Area** will appear on the right of your Scratch screen:

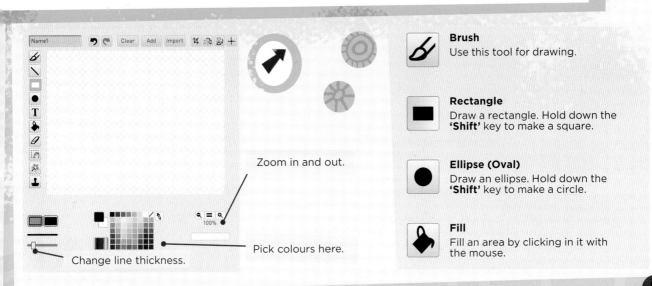

Zoom in and out.

Change line thickness.

Pick colours here.

Brush
Use this tool for drawing.

Rectangle
Draw a rectangle. Hold down the **'Shift'** key to make a square.

Ellipse (Oval)
Draw an ellipse. Hold down the **'Shift'** key to make a circle.

Fill
Fill an area by clicking in it with the mouse.

You get a call from Captain Maria, the brave explorer. She asks you to meet her at the Museum of Ancient Treasures ...

Welcome, old friend. After many years of searching, I have found an ancient map revealing the location of the Lost City of Gold, deep in the rainforest. I must travel there quickly to save its priceless treasures from robbers. But I cannot do it alone! Will you help me?

You agree to help Captain Maria on her dangerous journey! Before you set off, you must dress yourself in suitable clothing for an expedition.

GET READY...

1. Open **Scratch**.

Let's delete the cat sprite. In the **Sprites Pane, right click** the **cat**. On a Mac, hold the **'Ctrl'** key then **click**.

duplicate

delete

Choose **Delete**.

2. To start drawing yourself as an explorer, click the **Paint new sprite** button in the **Sprites Pane**.

3. Now you should be able to see the **Drawing Area**.

Choose the **Ellipse tool**.

At the bottom of the screen, click the **Solid ellipse**.

4. Select a **skin colour**.

Draw your head by dragging the mouse.

5. Choose the **Rectangle** tool and draw 2 rectangles for your arms and body.

50%

Make your explorer **half the width** of the Drawing Area.

6. Use rectangles to make your trousers and boots.

If things go wrong, click **Undo** and go back a step.

7. Choose the **Line tool**.

Set it to a **medium thickness**.

8. Draw a belt, then add 2 lines for the brim of your hat.

9. Choose the **Fill** tool then click the top of your head.

10. Use the **Brush** tool to add final details.

Now turn the page to find out how to save your explorer drawing so you can use it on your expedition. Quick – turn over!

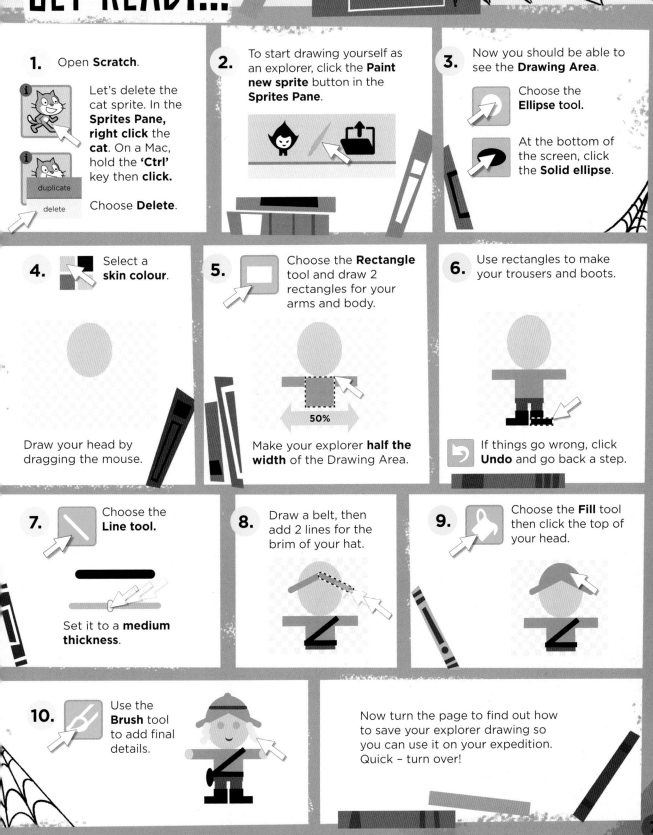

Oops. I packed a hamper of supplies for the trip, but I can't remember where I left it! Can you find it? I think it's somewhere in the museum ...

FIND THE FOOD

1. Before you do anything else, save your explorer sprite so you can use it for all the other activities in this book.

In the **Sprites Pane, right click** on the **explorer** sprite icon. On a Mac computer, hold the **'Ctrl'** key and **click**.

Click **Save to local file**.

Type in **explorer** as a name for your sprite and click **OK**.

2. In the centre of the screen, click the **Scripts** tab so Scratch is ready for you to add some code to make your explorer move.

3. Drag these blocks into the **Scripts Area**, in this order. Remember that the colour of each block tells us which group it is in. So the **'When green flag clicked'** block is in the **Events** group. The blue blocks are in the **Motion** group. All the purple blocks are in the **Looks** group. The **'Repeat'** loop block is in **Control**. You can click in the white box in a block in order to change the message or number, so click in the **'Think'** and **'Say'** blocks to type in the words.

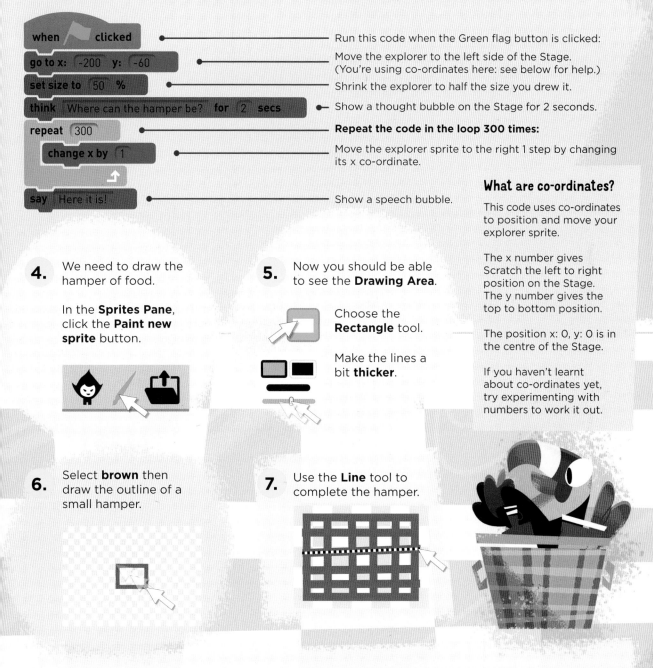

when ⚑ clicked — Run this code when the Green flag button is clicked:

go to x: -200 y: -60 — Move the explorer to the left side of the Stage. (You're using co-ordinates here: see below for help.)

set size to 50 % — Shrink the explorer to half the size you drew it.

think Where can the hamper be? for 2 secs — Show a thought bubble on the Stage for 2 seconds.

repeat 300 — **Repeat the code in the loop 300 times:**

change x by 1 — Move the explorer sprite to the right 1 step by changing its x co-ordinate.

say Here it is! — Show a speech bubble.

What are co-ordinates?

This code uses co-ordinates to position and move your explorer sprite.

The x number gives Scratch the left to right position on the Stage. The y number gives the top to bottom position.

The position x: 0, y: 0 is in the centre of the Stage.

If you haven't learnt about co-ordinates yet, try experimenting with numbers to work it out.

4. We need to draw the hamper of food.

In the **Sprites Pane**, click the **Paint new sprite** button.

5. Now you should be able to see the **Drawing Area**.

Choose the **Rectangle** tool.

Make the lines a bit **thicker**.

6. Select **brown** then draw the outline of a small hamper.

7. Use the **Line** tool to complete the hamper.

8. Drag the hamper to the **right side** of the Stage. Then click the **Green flag** button at the top right of the **Stage**. Your explorer should find Captain Maria's lost hamper!

To save your code, click the **File** menu, then **Download to your computer**. Then to use it again, you can click **File** and **Upload from your computer**.

Captain Maria takes you into the museum gardens, where her hot-air balloon is waiting ...

DISASTER! My hot-air balloon has been punctured. We can't take off for the rainforest until it is fixed!

Fix Captain Maria's balloon by drawing your own hot-air balloon sprite.

HOT-AIR BALLOON

90%

Your drawing should be **almost as tall** as the Drawing Area. If not, your games might not work. If things go wrong, click **Undo**.

1. Start a new Scratch file.

Delete the cat sprite. In the **Sprites Pane**, **right click** the cat. On a Mac, hold the **'Ctrl'** key then **click.**

Click **Delete.**

2. Start drawing your balloon by clicking the **Paint new sprite** button in the **Sprites Pane**.

You should now see the **Drawing Area.**

3. Choose the **Ellipse** tool.

At the bottom of the screen, click the **Solid ellipse.**

10

4.  Select **red**.

Draw a large oval in the top centre of the Drawing Area.

5. 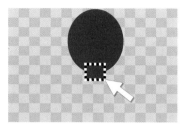 Choose the **Rectangle** tool.

Add a small rectangle.

6. Select **brown** and draw the basket.

7. Choose the **Line** tool.

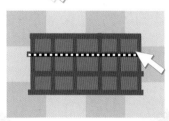 Make the line **thicker**. Add some detail.

8. Draw two **yellow** lines across the balloon.

9. Draw **brown** lines to join the balloon to the basket.

10. Use the **Zoom** control so you can add small details more easily. Zoom in for the next step.

200%

Zoom out   Zoom in

11.  Use the **Brush** tool to draw yourself and Maria.

12.

Decorate the balloon!

13. Now save your balloon sprite so you can use it to take off ...

In the Sprites Pane, **right click** your **balloon**. On a Mac, hold **'Ctrl'** and **click**.

delete
save to local file

Click **Save to local file**.

Type in **balloon** as a name for your sprite and click **OK**.

Thank you for fixing my balloon! Climb aboard and we can go ...

UP, UP AND AWAY!

1. Start a new Scratch file.

File▼

⬁ New

Right click the **cat**. On a Mac, hold **'Ctrl'** and **click**.

⬁ Click **Delete**.

duplicate
delete

2. You need to upload the hot-air balloon sprite you drew on the previous page. If you haven't already drawn it, turn back to page 10 and follow steps 2 to 13.

In the **Sprites Pane**, click **Upload sprite from file**.

```
My Documents
game.sb2
maze.sb2
balloon.sprite2
                OK
```

Find your file and click **OK**.

The sprite will appear in the Sprites Pane.

Sprite1

3. Click the **Scripts** tab and drag this code into the **Scripts Area** to make your balloon fly.

Scripts

```
when [flag] clicked
go to x: 0  y: -85
set size to 40 %
forever
    point towards mouse-pointer ▼
    move 1 steps
    point in direction 90 ▼
```

— Run the code below when the Green flag button is clicked:

— Start the balloon at the centre bottom of the Stage.

— Shrink the balloon to 40% of the size you drew it.

— **Repeat the code in the loop forever:**

— Make the balloon point towards the mouse pointer.

— Move the balloon forwards 1 step.

— Keep the balloon upright by making it point to the right.

4. Now we will draw a background for our balloon to take off in front of.

In the **Sprites Pane**, click the **Stage** icon.

Click the **Backdrops** tab.

Select the **Fill** tool.

Choose **light blue**.

Fill in the background by clicking in the **Drawing Area**.

5. Now let's draw some grass on the ground.

Select the **Rectangle** tool.

At the bottom of the screen, click the **Solid rectangle**.

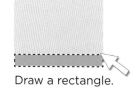

Choose **dark green**.

Draw a rectangle.

6. Now click the **Green flag** button to test your code. Move your mouse pointer around and the balloon will fly slowly towards it. It's time to take off for the rainforest!

Remember to save your game by clicking the **File** menu then **Download to your computer**.

As you fly through the Mysterious Mountains, your skills are put to the test yet again ...

We are going to crash into the mountain! Steer us into that cave and — hopefully — out the other side.

CAVE CRASH

1. Start a new file.

File ▾

New

Delete the **cat** sprite.

duplicate

delete

2. Now we will draw our cave.

Stage
1 Backdrop

Click the **Stage** button in the **Sprites Pane**.

Backdrops

Click the **Backdrops** tab.

Select the **Fill** tool.

Choose **dark brown**.

Click in the **Drawing Area** to fill it.

3. Choose the **Line** tool.

Choose **dark grey**.

Make the line width **thicker**.

Draw the bottom of the cave.

4. Use lines to draw the top of the cave.

Leave a gap between the top and bottom!

5. Colour in the cave with the **Fill** tool.

If the colour leaks out, click **Undo** and draw a line over any gaps.

6. To upload your balloon sprite, click **Upload sprite from file**.

My Documents
game.sb2
maze.sb2
balloon.sprite2
OK

Find your file and click **OK**.

The sprite will appear.

Sprite1

7. Click **Scripts** then add this code to make the balloon fly until it hits the rocks in the cave. You will find the **'Touching colour'** block in the **Sensing** group. Drop it in the hole in the **'Repeat until'** loop.

Scripts

How to set the colour for a 'Touching' block

Click the colour square.

touching color ?

The pointer changes.

On the Stage, click the colour you want to check for.

The colour is now set.

touching color ?

when ⚑ clicked — Run the code below when the Green flag button is clicked:

set size to 15 % — Shrink the balloon to 15% of its size.

go to x: -220 y: 0 — Move it to the left side of the Stage.

repeat until touching color ? — **Repeat this code until the balloon hits grey rock:**

point towards mouse-pointer ▼ — Point it towards the mouse pointer.

move 1 steps — Move forwards 1 step.

point in direction 90▼ — Keep it upright.

repeat 90 — **If rock is hit, repeat this code 90 times:**

turn ↻ 8 degrees — Rotate the balloon 8 degrees.

change y by -4 — Move it down.

8. Click the **Green flag** button to fly safely through the cave!

At last you are soaring above the rainforest. But so are thousands of bloodthirsty bats!

Argh! We must escape these deadly vampire bats! Nowwww!

BAT ATTACK

1. Start a new file and **delete** the **cat** sprite.

duplicate

delete

2. Now we will draw a sky background for our balloon to fly through.

Stage
1 Backdrop

In the **Sprites Pane**, click the **Stage** icon.

Backdrops

Click the **Backdrops** tab.

Select the **Fill** tool.

Click **blue**.

Fill in the background.

3.

To upload your balloon sprite, click **Upload sprite from file**.

My Documents
game.sb2
maze.sb2
balloon.sprite2

OK

Find your file and click **OK**.

Sprite1

The sprite will appear.

4. Drag this code into the **Scripts Area** to make the **hot-air balloon** fly.

when ⚑ clicked	———— Run the code below when the Green flag button is clicked:
go to x: -200 y: 0	———— Start the balloon on the left of the Stage.
set size to 25 %	———— Shrink it to 25% of its size.
forever	———— **Repeat the code in the loop forever:**
point towards mouse-pointer ▼	———— Make the balloon point towards the mouse pointer.
move 1 steps	———— Move the balloon forwards 1 step.
point in direction 90 ▼	———— Keep the balloon upright.

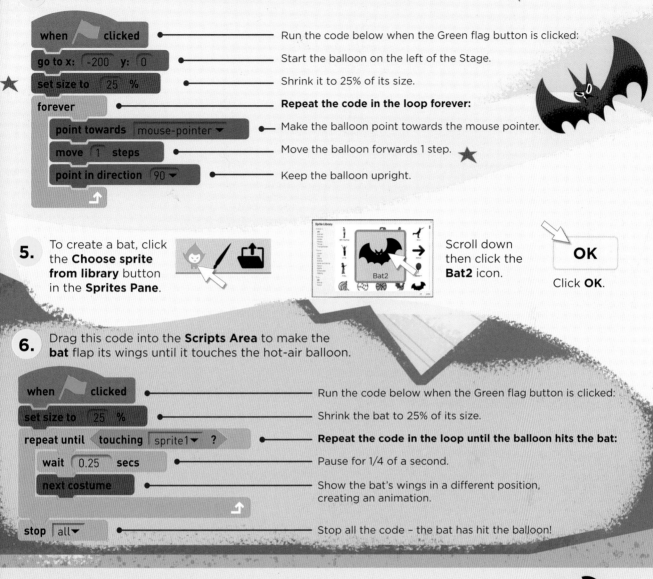

5. To create a bat, click the **Choose sprite from library** button in the **Sprites Pane**.

Scroll down then click the **Bat2** icon.

OK

Click **OK**.

6. Drag this code into the **Scripts Area** to make the **bat** flap its wings until it touches the hot-air balloon.

when ⚑ clicked	———— Run the code below when the Green flag button is clicked:
set size to 25 %	———— Shrink the bat to 25% of its size.
repeat until ◇ touching sprite1 ▼ ?	———— **Repeat the code in the loop until the balloon hits the bat:**
wait 0.25 secs	———— Pause for 1/4 of a second.
next costume	———— Show the bat's wings in a different position, creating an animation.
stop all ▼	———— Stop all the code – the bat has hit the balloon!

How the bat animation works

The animation works in a similar way to a cartoon on the TV or in a movie. By switching quickly between different images, we make it look as if the sprite is moving.

Costume 1

The bat sprite has two 'costumes'. Each costume is slightly different: one has the wings up, one has them down. Changing the costumes quickly makes it look as if the bat is flying!

Costume 2

7. **Right click** (**'Ctrl' click** on a Mac) the bat and choose **Duplicate**.

info

duplicate

8. Drag the new bat into a space.

9. Repeat step 7 to add more bats.

Now click the **Green flag**!

17

You touch down in the rainforest, hopefully not too far from the fabled City of Gold. Captain Maria wades into a murky-looking river ...

YIKES! THE WATER IS INFESTED WITH DEADLY ANACONDAS!

You must cross the river to reach the City of Gold, so you have no choice but to wade in after Captain Maria. Make sure you avoid the anacondas.

CROSS THE RIVER

1. Start a new file. **Delete** the **cat** sprite.

duplicate

delete

2. Backdrops

Click **Backdrops**.

Select the **Fill** tool.

Click **dark green**.

Fill in the background.

3. Now we need to draw the river.

Select the **Brush** tool.

Click **blue**.

Make the brush width **thicker**.

Draw one side of the river.

Next draw the other side.

Fill in the river.

Choose **green** and use the **Brush** to draw small islands.

4. Let's draw a deadly anaconda.

Click the **Paint new sprite** button.

The anaconda must be about **three-quarters of the width** of the Drawing Area.

75%

Choose **red** and select the **Brush** tool.

Make the brush **very thick**.

Draw the snake's body.

Add a head.

Make the brush **thinner** to draw eyes and a tongue.

5. Click the **Scripts** tab and drag this code into the **Scripts Area** to make the **anaconda** swim.

when [flag] clicked ●————— Run the code below when the Green flag is clicked:

set size to 20 % ●————— Shrink the anaconda to 20% of its size.

forever ●————— **Repeat the code in the loop forever:**

move 1 steps ●————— Move the anaconda forwards 1 step.

if on edge, bounce ●————— If it reaches the edge of the Stage, come back the other way.

Click the **Green flag** to test your code. You may need to drag the snake into the river. It should then swim slowly from side to side.

6. When the anaconda swims back, it will be upside down. To fix this, do the following:

Sprite1

In the **Sprites Pane**, click the blue **i**.

rotation style ↻ ↔ ●

Set the **rotation style** of the anaconda to the centre option, **left-right**.

Click the **blue triangle** button when you have finished.

7. Make some more anacondas. **Right click** (or '**Ctrl**' click) the anaconda and choose **Duplicate**.

info

duplicate

8. **Drag** the new anaconda into a space.

Repeat step 7 until you have around **6** snakes.

9. Upload your **explorer** sprite by clicking **Upload sprite from file**.

Find your file and click **OK**.

My Documents
game.sb2
maze.sb2
explorer.sprite2
OK

The sprite will appear.

Sprite7

10. Click the **Scripts** tab and drag this code into the **Scripts Area** for the **explorer** sprite.

```
when [flag] clicked
```
Run the code below when the Green flag button is clicked:

```
show
```
Make sure the explorer sprite is visible.

```
set size to 20 %
```
Shrink the explorer to 20% of its size.

```
go to x: 0 y: 160
```
Start the explorer at the top centre of the Stage.

```
wait until    touching color [ ] ?
```
Wait until the explorer is touching a snake
(for help with this block, turn to page 15, step 7):

```
say Aggghhh! for 2 secs
```
Then show a message for 2 seconds.

```
hide
```
Make the explorer disappear. (Whoops, you've been eaten!)

11. Now add these 4 separate groups of code (called 'scripts') for the **explorer**.
Each of the scripts runs when a different arrow key is pressed on the keyboard.
Each script changes either the x co-ordinate (how far across the Stage the sprite
is) or the y co-ordinate (how far up it is).

```
when up arrow ▼ key pressed
```
When the **'Up'** arrow key is pressed:

```
change y by 5
```
Move the explorer up 5 steps.

```
when left arrow ▼ key pressed
change x by -5
```

```
when right arrow ▼ key pressed
change x by 5
```

```
when down arrow ▼ key pressed
change y by -5
```

12. Use the **arrow** keys to move your explorer
across the river. Avoid the anacondas!

You trudge through the rainforest until, between the trees, you glimpse it ... the **City of Gold**!

I can hardly believe my eyes! After all these years of searching ... Priceless treasures are hidden inside that golden pyramid. Let's go inside! The only problem is that monkey guarding the entrance. He looks a little bit annoyed ...

MUNKEY MADNESS

Can you climb to the top of the pyramid, avoiding the bananas thrown by the furious monkey?

1. Start a new file and **delete** the **cat** sprite.

2. Let's start to draw a background for our game.

Click **Backdrops**.

Select the **Fill** tool.

Click **light blue**.

Choose **Gradient fill**.

Fill the background by clicking in the Drawing Area.

3. Draw some grass on the ground.

Select the **Rectangle** tool.

Click the **Solid rectangle**.

Choose **dark green**.

Draw a rectangle.

4. Now draw the golden pyramid.

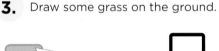

Select the **Rectangle** tool.

Choose **yellow**.

Carefully draw the first level.

If it is not in exactly the right place, use the handles to move it.

Draw **4** more rectangles to add each level of the pyramid. If a rectangle is not in the correct place, adjust it with the handles or click **Undo**.

5. Draw the path that leads to the top of the pyramid.

Select the **Rectangle** tool.

Choose the **golden** colour below the yellow.

Carefully draw a path on the pyramid.

If a rectangle is not in exactly the right place, use the handles to move it or use the **Undo** button and try again.

Add rectangles in the pattern shown here to complete the path to the top. In the end, your temple should look like this!

6. To create the monkey, click the **Choose sprite from library** button.

Scroll down then click the **Monkey1** icon.

Click **OK**.

Monkey1

OK

7. Click the **Shrink** button in the Scratch **Menu bar**, then click the monkey on the **Stage** several times to make it much smaller.

Drag the monkey to the **top** of the pyramid.

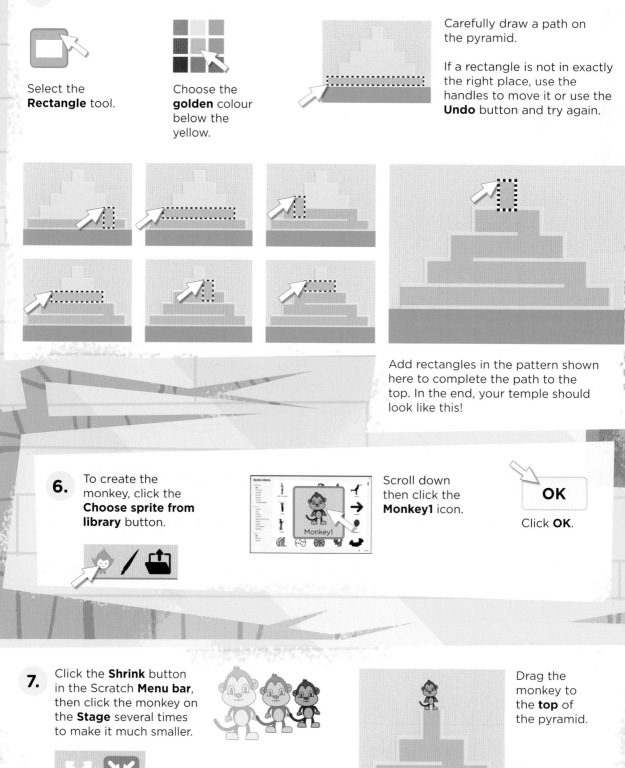

8. To give the monkey his bananas, click the **Choose sprite from library** button.

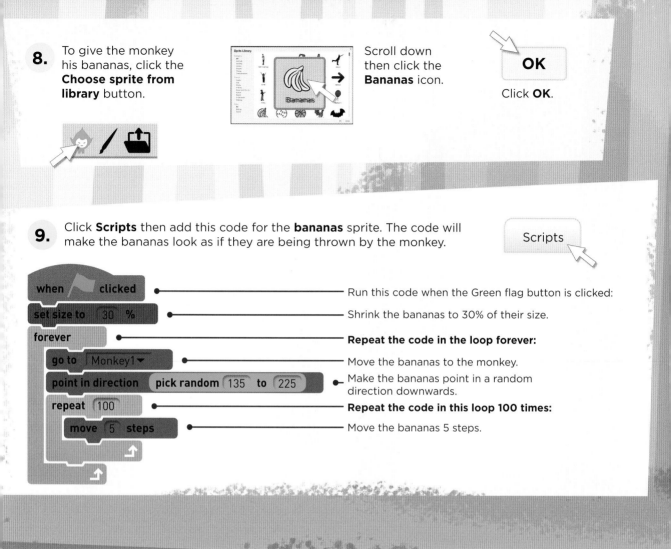

Scroll down then click the **Bananas** icon.

Click **OK**.

9. Click **Scripts** then add this code for the **bananas** sprite. The code will make the bananas look as if they are being thrown by the monkey.

Scripts

```
when [flag] clicked
set size to 30 %
forever
  go to Monkey1 ▼
  point in direction (pick random 135 to 225)
  repeat 100
    move 5 steps
```

Run this code when the Green flag button is clicked:

Shrink the bananas to 30% of their size.

Repeat the code in the loop forever:

Move the bananas to the monkey.

Make the bananas point in a random direction downwards.

Repeat the code in this loop 100 times:

Move the bananas 5 steps.

Setting a random direction

```
point in direction (pick random 1 to 10)
```

The **'Pick random'** block is in the **Operators** group. It commands Scratch to pick a random number between the two numbers you type into its holes.

Drag the block from its left-hand side. As you drag it over the white circle on the **'Point in direction'** block, the border will glow to show it is in the right place.

10. To upload your explorer sprite, click **Upload sprite from file**.

My Documents
game.sb2
maze.sb2
explorer.sprite2
OK

Find your file and click **OK**.

Sprite1

The sprite will appear.

11. Click **Scripts** then add this code to control the **explorer** sprite. (There are 3 different sprites in this game, so make sure you've got the right one selected in the **Sprites Pane**.)

Scripts

```
when [flag] clicked
set size to 15 %
go to x: -220 y: -140
repeat until    touching  Monkey1 ▼ ?
    if  touching color [ ] ?    then
        turn C 180 degrees
        move 5 steps

    if  touching  Bananas ▼ ?  then
        say OW! for 2 secs
        go to x: -220 y: -140

say Well done, now go inside! for 2 secs
```

Run the code below when the Green flag button is clicked:

Shrink the explorer to 15% of its size.

Move the explorer to the left-hand side of the pyramid.

Repeat the code in the loop until the explorer reaches the monkey at the top of the pyramid:
If the explorer hits the edge of the path (click on the edge of the pyramid to set the colour), run this code:
Turn the explorer round 180 degrees.

Move 5 steps.

If the explorer gets hit by a banana, run this code:

Show a message for 2 seconds.

Move the explorer to the bottom of the pyramid.

When the explorer reaches the monkey at the top, show a message and stop the game.

12. Now add these four separate scripts. They will make the explorer move up, down, left or right when you use the arrow keys on your keyboard.

```
when up arrow ▼ key pressed
point in direction 0 ▼
move 5 steps
```

When the **'Up'** arrow key is pressed:

Point the explorer upwards.

Move it up 5 steps.

```
when left arrow ▼ key pressed
point in direction -90 ▼
move 5 steps
```

```
when right arrow ▼ key pressed
point in direction 90 ▼
move 5 steps
```

When the **'Right'** arrow key is pressed:

Point the explorer right.

Move it right 5 steps.

```
when down arrow ▼ key pressed
point in direction 180 ▼
move 5 steps
```

When the **'Down'** arrow key is pressed:

Point the explorer downwards.

Move it down 5 steps.

13. We need to change the way the explorer moves so it does not rotate when it changes direction (we want it to stay upright!).

In the **Sprites Pane**, click the blue **i** circle on the **explorer** icon.

Set the **rotation style** to the right-hand option, **no-rotate**.

Now click the **blue triangle** button.

14. Press the **Green flag** button to battle the angry monkey!

Don't forget to save your game by choosing **File** and **Download to your computer**.

Not fitting in?

If your paths are too thin, the explorer may not be able to fit through them.

If so, reduce the percentage in the **'Set size to'** block in step 11. Try **12%** or less.

HURRAY! LET'S GO INSIDE!

OOH OOH AAH AAH!

You enter the pyramid. It is dark and you are not alone ...

OoooOooOH

Help me collect the treasure, old friend. There is nothing to fear here!

MAZE OF GOLD

Collect the treasure, but avoid the ghostly ghoul!

1. Start a new file and **delete** the **cat** sprite.

duplicate

delete

2. Draw a pyramid on the backdrop, just like on page 23, steps 2–4.

3. Select the **Rectangle** tool.

Choose **black**.

Carefully draw a corridor from the top of the pyramid.

Add more corridors to complete your maze. Make sure they are not too small for the explorer to fit through.

4. Now upload your **explorer** sprite.

Click **Upload sprite from file**. Find your file and click **OK**.

5. Add a ghost to haunt the corridors. Click **Choose sprite from library**.

Click **Ghoul**.

Click **OK**.

6. Click **Scripts** then add this code to make the **ghoul** move around the pyramid.

Scripts

when 🏴 clicked	⟶ Run this code when the Green flag is clicked:
go to `random position▼`	⟶ Move the ghoul to a random place on the Stage.
set `ghost▼` effect to `50`	⟶ Create a special effect (called 'ghost') which will make the ghoul partly invisible.
set size to `25` %	⟶ Shrink the ghoul to 25% of its size.
forever	⟶ **Repeat the code in the loop forever:**
move `1` steps	⟶ Move the ghoul forwards one step.

Now add this separate script, which will change the direction of the ghoul every 5 seconds.

when 🏴 clicked	⟶ Run this code when the Green flag is clicked:
forever	⟶ **Repeat the code in the loop forever:**
wait `5` secs	⟶ Wait for 5 seconds.
point towards `Sprite1▼`	⟶ Then point the ghoul towards the explorer.

7. We will stop the **explorer** sprite from turning upside down when it changes direction.

Sprite1

In the **Sprites Pane**, click the blue **i**.

rotation style ↻ ↔

Set the **rotation style** to the right-hand option, **no-rotate**.

Click the **blue triangle** button.

8. Let's count how many coins we find. We'll use a special part of our program, called a variable. Variables are a way that programs store values that can change – such as the score.

Sound
Pen
Data

Click the **Data** group.

Make a Variable

Click **Make a variable**.

Variable name: `score`

Call it **score**.

OK

Click **OK**.

9. Click the **Scripts** tab and add this code for the **explorer** sprite. The orange blocks are in the **Data** group. The green **'Equals (=)'** block is in the **Operators** group. Drop the little **'Score'** block into it.

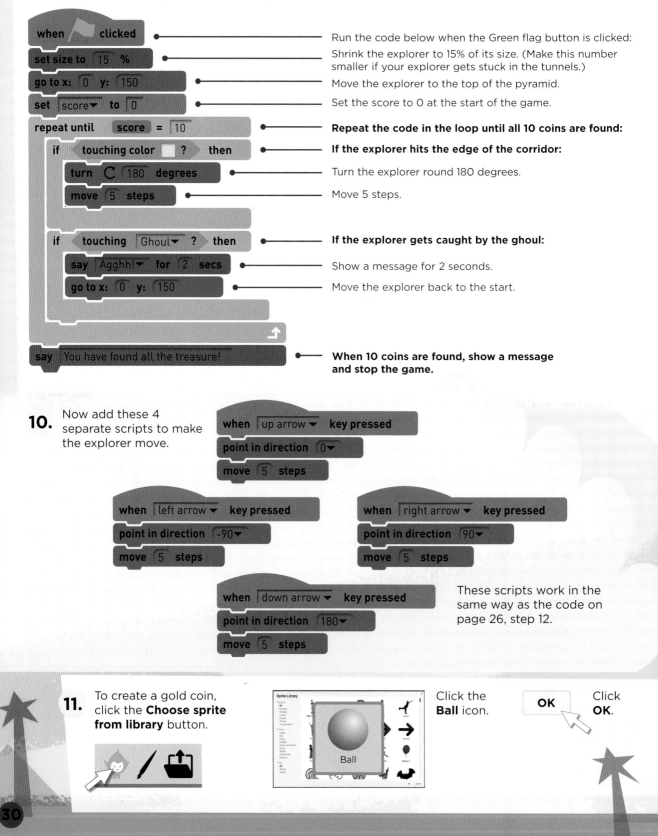

when ▶ clicked — Run the code below when the Green flag button is clicked:

set size to 15 % — Shrink the explorer to 15% of its size. (Make this number smaller if your explorer gets stuck in the tunnels.)

go to x: 0 y: 150 — Move the explorer to the top of the pyramid.

set score▼ to 0 — Set the score to 0 at the start of the game.

repeat until score = 10 — **Repeat the code in the loop until all 10 coins are found:**

  if touching color ☐ ? then — **If the explorer hits the edge of the corridor:**

    turn ↻ 180 degrees — Turn the explorer round 180 degrees.

    move 5 steps — Move 5 steps.

  if touching Ghoul▼ ? then — **If the explorer gets caught by the ghoul:**

    say Agghh!▼ for 2 secs — Show a message for 2 seconds.

    go to x: 0 y: 150 — Move the explorer back to the start.

say You have found all the treasure! — **When 10 coins are found, show a message and stop the game.**

10. Now add these 4 separate scripts to make the explorer move.

when up arrow ▼ key pressed
point in direction 0▼
move 5 steps

when left arrow ▼ key pressed
point in direction -90▼
move 5 steps

when right arrow ▼ key pressed
point in direction 90▼
move 5 steps

when down arrow ▼ key pressed
point in direction 180▼
move 5 steps

These scripts work in the same way as the code on page 26, step 12.

11. To create a gold coin, click the **Choose sprite from library** button.

Click the **Ball** icon.

OK — Click **OK**.

12. Click **Scripts** and add this code to make the **coin** disappear when the explorer finds it.

Scripts

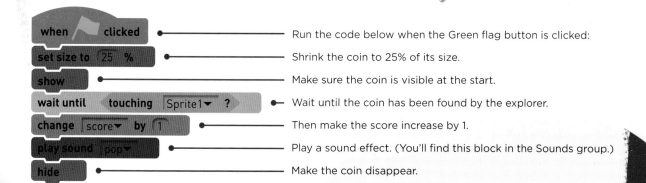

when ⚑ clicked — Run the code below when the Green flag button is clicked:

set size to 25 % — Shrink the coin to 25% of its size.

show — Make sure the coin is visible at the start.

wait until touching Sprite1▼ ? — Wait until the coin has been found by the explorer.

change score▼ by 1 — Then make the score increase by 1.

play sound pop▼ — Play a sound effect. (You'll find this block in the Sounds group.)

hide — Make the coin disappear.

13. In the **Sprites Pane**, **right click** (or **'Ctrl' click**) the **Ball** sprite. Choose **Duplicate**.

14. Drag the new coin into a gap in the corridors. You may find it easier to do this after pressing the **Green flag** to shrink the coins.

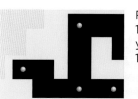

Repeat step 13 until you have 10 coins.

15. Click the **Green flag** to collect all the gold. Don't forget to save your game.

Thank you for all your help! Without you, I could never have reached the city. Let's take these coins back to the Museum of Ancient Treasures.

GLOSSARY

Animation – A series of pictures shown one after the other to give the illusion of movement (for example, that a sprite is walking).

Code – A series of instructions or commands.

Command – A word or code block that tells the computer what to do.

Co-ordinates – The position of an object determined by its x (centre to right) and y (centre to top) values.

Data group – The set of Scratch code blocks that control and access variables.

Degree – The unit measuring the angle that an object turns.

Drawing Area – The part of the right-hand side of the Scratch screen that is used to draw sprites and backgrounds.

Duplicate – A simple way to create a copy of a sprite in Scratch.

Events group – The set of Scratch code blocks that are triggered when particular events happen, such as a key being pressed.

If then – A common form of selection in coding, where command(s) are run if something is true.

Language – A system of commands (in the form of blocks, words or numbers) that tell a computer how to do things.

Loop – A sequence of code blocks repeated a number of times.

Operators group – The set of Scratch code blocks that deals with calculations and comparing values.

Program – The set of commands that tell a computer how to do something such as play a game.

Scratch – A computer language that uses blocks of code to make a program.

Scripts Area – The part of the right-hand side of the Scratch screen to which code blocks are dragged to create programs.

Sensing group – The set of Scratch code blocks that detect when specific keys are pressed or where the mouse is.

Speed – How fast an object moves forwards. In Scratch, we use minus speed values to move objects backwards.

Sprite – An object that moves around the screen.

Sprites Pane – Part of the lower left of the Scratch screen where you select a sprite to add code to or change its appearance.

Stage – The area at the top left of the Scratch screen where you can watch your sprites move about.

Variable – A value or piece of information stored by a computer program. In computer games, a variable is commonly used to store the score.

INDEX